William C. Snow

The War of 1812

A Part of its Naval History

William C. Snow

The War of 1812
A Part of its Naval History

ISBN/EAN: 9783337115791

Printed in Europe, USA, Canada, Australia, Japan

Cover: Foto ©ninafisch / pixelio.de

More available books at **www.hansebooks.com**

THE WAR OF 1812.

A PART OF ITS NAVAL HISTORY. RECORDED AT THE TIME
BY A RHODE ISLAND CITIZEN.

The compiler of the following tables, Deacon William C.
Snow, was born in Providence in 1794, and died there in 1872.
His grandfather was a brother of the Rev. Joseph Snow, who
was the first pastor of the Beneficent Congregational Church
of this city. Mr. Snow was, during a period of his boyhood,
a pupil of the Rev. James Wilson, who succeeded the Rev.
Joseph Snow as pastor of that church. He was nearly related
to Capt. Samuel Snow of the Continental Army, who was
long an officer of the Rhode Island Society of the Cincinnati
and was in the early part of this century U. S. Consul at
Canton, China. Deacon Snow compiled these tables while
serving as a clerk in the Providence Post Office, at first under
Benjamin West, the celebrated almanac-maker of that period,
and then under the latter's son-in-law, Captain Gabriel Allen,*
who served in the Revolutionary War and was a member of
the Rhode Island Society of the Cincinnati. The post office
was then kept in the old building that has long been known
as Turk's Head. Deacon Snow left a son, J. Lippitt Snow,
worthy of his heritage, a man honored and beloved in life and
his memory cherished by a wide circle of friends.

The paper is printed verbatim, without note or comment. It
was submitted several months ago to a member of this society,
Albert Holbrook, Esq., who would have added much to its

---

*Memoirs of Captain Gabriel Allen and Samuel Snow, will, it is pre-
sumed, soon appear in the "Register of the Rhode Island Society of the
Cincinnati," compiled and edited by the Secretary-General of this insti-
tution, inaugurated at the disbandment of the Continental army in 1783.

interest if his life had been spared. Mr. Holbrook long made the maritime commerce of Rhode Island a special study, and he thus acquired some acquaintance with many officers and vessels named in this paper. He knew well the families and the public careers of Commodore Esek Hopkins and of Captain Abraham Whipple. On being shown Deacon Snow's paper, he expressed interest in it and also astonishment at the extent of our naval force at that time. He regretted that this paper had not been seen by Dr. Usher Parsons, the historian of Perry's Lake Erie expedition. He spoke in complimentary terms of what the Hon. William P. Sheffield had done to make known the privateers and corsairs manned by Rhode Islanders during our Revolutionary period.

As a man of integrity and business capacity the compiler of these tables needs no endorsement. He is well known, having been for a long series of years the successful agent of the Dyeing, Bleaching and Calendering Company, on Aborn Street, Providence. He rarely failed to accomplish what he undertook. He was a member of this society from 1858 till his death, in 1872. A necrological notice of him is given in the society's " Proceedings" of 1872-73. In early life he noted and recorded important facts, and at a later period helped make the history of his native town. Some of his manuscripts that were kept in a trunk with manuscripts left by the late Col. John Singer Dexter of the Continental Army, were submitted to devouring flames, as told to the writer of this note, to get the use of the trunk and to be spared the trouble of exhibiting the contents of the trunk to inquisitive visitors. A large, well-framed likeness of Deacon Snow is in the cabinet.

The paper is printed in the hope of drawing from their pigeon-holes or dark places in old boxes or trunks, other papers of the same general characters and of eliciting comments from students of this branch of history. The work in manuscript consists of forty-two folio pages, enclosed in a brown paper cover, labeled : " Providence, R. I., August 19, 1812. Prize Book. List of Privateers, etc., 1812."

There is reason to believe that many papers of equal historical interest and value are stowed away in dark attics, —papers
that will sooner or later be submitted to the flames or consigned to the junk shop, unless rescued by some historical
student or antiquarian. This paper has been so long neglected
or illtreated, either by its author or by this society,—perhaps by
both,—that it is *dog-eared*, and some names and figures are, here
and there, lost. The compiler gives notice that privateers with
this mark (*) have been taken. The ports where many of the
privateers belonged are stated in Deacon Snow's list of 446
prizes. Most of prizes were taken by privateers mentioned in
this table. See pp. 145 & 146.—[EDITOR.]

LIST OF PRIVATEERS, THEIR NAMES, NUMBER OF MEN, GUNS,
FITTED OUT IN DIFFERENT PORTS OF THE U. S. AMERICA,
SINCE THE DECLARATION OF WAR AGAINST ENGLAND, JUNE
18, 1812:

Privateers.	Captains.	Guns.	Men.
Teazer	Dobson	3	50
Paul Jones	Hazard	17	120
Marengo	Ridios	7	50
Eagle	Beauron	1	45
Rosamond	Campan	12	132
Benj. Franklin	Ingersol	8	120
Black Jake	Brown	2	60
Rover	Ferris	1	35
Ord's in Council	Howard	16	120
Saratoga	Vicker	18	140
United we Stand	Storey	2	50
Divided we Fall	Cropsey	2	50
Gov. Tompkins	Skinner	14	43
Retaliation	Newson	6	100
Spitfire	Miller	2	54
Gen. Armstrong	Bernard	18	140
Jack's Favorite	Johnston	4	80
Yorktown	Storey	18	160
Tartar	King	6	80
Holkar	Rowland	16	150
Anaconda	Shaler	16	160
Patriot	Merihew	2	50
Union	Hicks	1	24
Turn Over	Southmead	1	16
Right of Search. ——		1	50
Bunker Hill	Lewis	4	*60
Madison*	——	1	....
Atlas	Moffatt	..	....
Tickler	Johnson	..	....
Nonpareil	Martin	..	....
Jefferson*	Kahew	..	....
Snow Bird	Stacy	..	....
Fair Trader	Morgan	..	....
Buckskin*	Bray	..	....
Lion	——	..	....
Dolphin	Endicott	..	....
Sarah Anne	Moon	1	42
Mary Ann	Chazel	..	....
John	Crowninshields	16	105
Fame	Webb	..	....
Polly	Handy	..	....
Matilda	——	..	....
Gov. McKean	Lucett	..	....
Swallow†	Burch	5	80

*Those with this mark have been taken.
†Sparrow.

Names.	Captains.	Guns.	Men.
Active*	Patterson..	2	22
Spencer	Morse	..	....
Comet	Boyle	12	120
Gossamer*	Goodrich ..	14	....
Orlando	——	6	40
Dart	Green	..	....
Nancy	Smart	..	....
Tom	Wilson	14	100
Leader	Avery	2	20
America	Richard ...	22	200
Yankee	Wilson	18	120
Actress*	——	4	53
Intention*	——.....	1	29
Gleaner*	——	8	50
Catharine*	Burnham ..	14	....
Curlew*	——	..	....
Com. Barry*	Elliott	6	....
Mars*	Brooks	..	....
—— ——	Hazard	17	....
Globe	Murphy ...	7	90
Rapid	Crabtree...	..	....
Wiley Reinard	..——	..	....
Regulator	Mansfield ..	..	....
Alfred	——	16	13
Decatur*	Nicholls ...	..	....
Argus*	——	..	....
High Flyer	Gavett	7	10
Rossie	Barney	13	....
Wasp	Taylor	1	50
Eagle	Daniels....	..	....
Bona	Dameron ..	6	80
Hornet	Frost	..	....
Dash	Caraway...	..	....
Mars	Bulkley	..	....
Squando	Watson	..	....
Success	Dennis	..	....
Poor Sailor	..——	..	....
Hazard	Dennis	..	....
Thomas	Shaw	14	100
Science	——	..	....
Industry	Mudge	..	....
Nonsuch	Lively	12	100
Montgomery	Breed	14	112
Thrasher	Parsons ...	18	115
Bee	Masabau ..	..	....
Dromo	Cooper	..	....

In addition to the privateers sailed from Balimore, are 25 letter of Marque schooners, fast sailers, carrying from 6 to 10 guns each and from 30 to 50 men each besides officers.‡

Names.	Captains.	Guns.	Men.
Revenge	Miller	14	140
Yankee †	Brooks	2	60
Contradiction	Pascal	.	....
Alexander	Welman ...	16	155
Thorn	Hooper	18	148
Joel Barlow	——	..	....
Providence*	Hopkins ...	6	58
Rambler	——	..	....
Hiram †	Wilson	6	40
Swift	Topham ...	..	....
Brothers	——	..	....
Plough Boy	——	..	....
Baltimore	Veazy	..	....
Gov. Gerry	——	..	....
Yankee Lass	Sweet	12	100
Lovely Lass	Smith	5	30
Dolphin	Stafford ...	10	100
Rolla	Dooley	5	80
Joseph & Mary	Wescott ...	4	83
Liberty	Pratt	1	50
Hornet †	Frost	1	50
First Consul	——	..	....
Snap Dragon	Pasteur....	7	100
Growler	Graves	..	....
Republican	Reynolds ..	..	....
Terrappin	——	..	....
Fox	Brown	..	....
G. Washinston	..——	..	....
Lilly	——	1	....
Hunter	——	..	....
Gallinipper	——	2	....
Gen. Greene	——	..	....
Fly	——	..	....
Cossack—from Salem		..	....
Little Dick	——	..	....
Blockade	——	..	....
Grand Turk	——	16	....
Young Teazer	Johnston...	5	....
"True Blooded Yankee," fitted out at Brest, France. }		20	200

Gen. Armstrong of Charleston; the other of the same name belongs at New York.

Decatur, Dixon, from Charleston, S. C.; the other of the same name, from Newburyport.

| Roger | Quardes ... | 14 | .... |
| Scourge | —— .... | 16 | .... |

†Lost : two of them.   * Taken.   ‡ These were set down but a few months after the War; there is now a great many from all parts of the Union.

LIST OF VESSELS CAPTURED BY THE AMERICANS SINCE THE DECLARATION OF WAR, JUNE 17, 1812.

RECORDED BY WM. C. SNOW, THEN A CLERK IN POST OFFICE, PROVIDENCE, R. I.

1. The schooner Patriot, I. A. Brown, master ; from Gaudaloup bound for Halifax with a valuable cargo of sugar, taken by the revenue cutter Jefferson, Wm. Ham, master, arrived here yesterday. Norfolk, June 26th.

2. A pilot boat laden with a large quantity of English goods has been seized by the collector at Eastport.

3. The brig Pickering, Davis, from Gibralter, was taken by the frigate Belvedera, and ordered to Halifax ; she was retaken when within six miles of Halifax light, by the crew, assisted by four of the prize crew and carried into Gloucester, Ms.

4. The Ontario, a fine new schooner of 87 tons, was taken by Capt. Turran, deputy collector, and brought into the port of St. Vincents, last week.

5. The Privateer Fame, Webb, of Boston, has taken a ship of near three hundred tons, laden with square timber.

6. Also by the same privateer, a brig of 200 tons burthen, laden with tar, arrived at Boston.

7. Arrived at Marblehead, a new English brig, 200 tons burthen, mounting 6 guns, prize to the Lion & Snow-bird privateer.

8, 9, 10. Three Novia Scotia Shallops with English & West india goods and some thousands of dollars in specie, prizes to the Lion privateer.

11, 12, 13. Three British schooners, with Plaister, lumber, & naval stores, corn, flour, &c., prizes to the privateer Jefferson ; two of them were taken out of beaver harbour by the enterprising crew of the Jefferson, in open day.

14. A large shallop laden with British prize goods, prize to the Jefferson Privateer.

15. British sloop Endeavour, with sugar, prize to the privateer Polly.

16. At Ogdensburgh, N. Y. Eleven batteaus with arms, and ammunition belonging to the british, captured on the river St. Lawrence.

17. At Salem, July 13. An English ship of 6 guns and 13 men, from England, with ammunition, arms, &c., for Novia Scotia, a prize to the Dolphin privateer.

18. The British Schooner Ann, Kelly, master, of Halifax, a prize to the Dolphin, with a cargo of Pork, wines, furs, cordage, &c.

19. The Dolphin has captured an English schooner from Halifax, and taking from her $1,000, released her.

20. British Ship Concord, prize to the privateer Fame.

21. A British brig from St. Andrews, bound to England, laden with flour, timber, &c., captured by the Dolphin.

22. Another British brig (name not known), prize to the Dolphin, has arrived.

23. Castine. The british brig Hero, from Lisbon, bound to St. Andrews, in ballast, prize to the privateer Teazer, of New York.

24. At Baltimore. The British schooner Fancy, Fogerty, bound from St. Croix to St. Andrews, with a cargo of sugars (vessel and cargo said to be worth 18,000 Dols.), a prize to the Dolphin, privateer.

25. At Cape Ann. A British ship of 300 tons, with flour, rice and naval stores, prize to the privateers Jefferson and Madison; the Jefferson lost one man during the attack on that vessel.

26. At Gloucester. The British Government Transport, No. 5, prize to the 1-gun privateer Madison, of that port, bound to St. Johns, under convoy of the Indian sloop-of-war, with 180 qr. casks gunpowder, 880 suits uniform for the 104th regiment British infantry, some bales of superfine cloths for officers' clothing, 10 casks wine, drums & other camp equipage, &c. She mounted two guns, had plenty of small arms & 12 men. The Transport is a fine brig of 295 tons, and is supposed with her cargo to be worth 50,000 Dollars.

27. At Charleston. Ship Roba & Betsy, London, 60 Days, seized by Lieut. Grandison, commander of the U. S. Guard Ship.

28. At Philadelphia. The brig Tulip, Capt. Monk, prize to the Atlas privateer.

29. At Baltimore. The British brig Lamphrey, from Jamaica, for Halifax, with rum, prize to the U. S. Frigate Essex.

30. Also taken by the U. S. Frigate Essex, a brig with 150 soldiers, ransomed the brig for a bill of Exchange of 14,000 Dols. on London, disarmed the men, &c., and released them on parole.

31, 32. Two English schooners from St. Johns, N. B., for Halifax, with full cargoes, prizes to the Snow Bird privateer.

33. At Wiscasset. A British schooner, with provisions, prize to the Fair trader.

34. At St. Mary's. The British schooner wade Johnston, from Nassau, with pine apples, Turtles, and 24,000 Dols. specie.

35. And the British schooner Pinder, from same port, with 10,000 Dols. prizes to the gunboats under Com. Campbell.

36. The English ship Ann Green, 460 tons burthen, with rum, coals, &c., carries 8 12-pound cannonades, and two long 6's, prize to the brig Gossamer. She has arrived.

37. A British schooner from Halifax, for Quebec, with naval & military stores, prize to the Buckskin privateer.

38. At Norfolk. A Bristol brig, from the West Indies, prize to the Paul Jones, privateer, of New York.

39. At Marblehead. A British schooner with Lumber and naval stores, prize to the Lion privateer.

40. July 17, in sight of Liverpool, N. B., captured the schooner Eliza, from Halifax, bound to Liverpool, with a quantity of Bottled Porter, stores, &c., by the privateer Buckskin.

41. Same day captured schooner Union Lass, in ballast, from Newfoundland, for Cape Sable, by the Buckskin.

42. At Boston. A British schooner of about 30 tons, with dry goods, sugar & rum, prize to a privateer.

43. An English brig from New Brunswick, for England, taken and burnt by Com. Roger's squadron.

44. Schooner Polly, from Sidney, for Halifax, with coal, prize to the Wiley Reynard. She is about 80 tons burthen.

45. Arrived at Chatham. An English brig from Jamaica, with a full cargo of rum, prize to the Bunker Hill privateer of New York.

46. The revenue Cutter Gallatin, McNeal, of Charleston, has captured a British Letter of Marque ship after a severe engagement of 8 hours, and taken her into Savannah.

47. Arrived at Savannah, July 24th, the revenue cutter James Madison, Capt. Brooks, with a British snow, mounting six 6-pounders with a quantity of small arms and ammunition. The letter of Marque was from Jamaica bound to England.

48. Arrived at Philadelphia, prize brig Elisabeth and Esther of Bermuda, late Kirkpatrick, master, sent in by the privateer Gov. McKean, Capt. Lucet of this port.

49. Arrived at New York, on Tuesday last, through the sound, the English ship Lady Sherbroke, James Wilson, prize master, a prize to the Marengo privateer of that port ; she was bound from Halifax to Kingston, Jamaica.

50, 51. Schooner Peggy from Sidney for Halifax, & a schooner from Cook's harbour to Halifax, prizes to the Wiley Reynard, arrived at Portland the 10th inst.

51 to 58 inclusive. The gunboats at St. Mary's have taken seven British and five Spanish Ships. ☞ The spanish ships are not counted.

59. Boston. Arrived at Salem, yesterday, Ship Venus, Ray, of New York, taken by the Dolphin privateer, laden with coal, crates, Dry goods, copper & white lead.

60. A New, light brig, prize to the John Privateer, bound from Gibraltar to Halifax.

61. A Schooner, prize to the John Privateer, from Jamaica with 160 puncheons rum.

62. Also a ship of 400 tons, coppered, in ballast from England, having eight 18-pounders. The John was left in chase of a ship of 400 tons from England with dry goods.

63. The Schooner Sally, from Cayenne, with a full cargo of Molasses, was sent into Newport on Saturday last by a privateer from that port.

64. Arrived at Baltimore, the fine British ship Henry, from St. Croix for London, taken by the privateer Comet, Capt Boyle, after an engagement of about 15 minutes. The ship mounted four 12-pounders and six 6-pounders, of the first class, coppered to the bends—400 tons burthen, and has a cargo of upwards of 700 hhds. of sugar, 13 pipes old Maderia wine and a quantity of Lignum Vitæ. Ship and cargo estimated at 150,000 Dollars.

65. Also schooner Alfred Leascome, from Bermuda for N. Providence, prize to privateer Spencer of Philadelphia; cargo, brandy, rum, claret wine, &c.

66. British schooner Eliza of Halifax, from Jamaica with 70 hhds. rum and fruit, arrived at Salem, prize to the privateer Polly.

67. A Ship from New Providence bound to London arrived in the Delaware, on Wednesday, the 12th inst., prize to the privateer Globe of Baltimore.

68. Also a brig from St. Domingo, for England, prize to the privateer Matilda of Philadelphia. The cargoes are said to consist of Dyewoods & coffee.

69. An English barque, prize to the ship Catharine of Boston, has arrived at Portland. She was captured 26th Ult., off Halifax, & The next morning, the Catharine engaged a gun brig. The action continued 45 minutes and ended with musketry & Pistols; coming on thick it was not ascertained which surrendered.

70. Boston, Aug. 18. The British brig James, from Halifax, has arrived at Falmouth, prize to the Bunker Hill privateer, Com. Jacob Lewis.

71. At Marblehead, American schooner Dinsmore, taken by the British Frigate Maidstone, retaken by a privateer out of Beverly.

72. At Gloucester, American schooner Three Brothers, taken by the above frigate and retaken by the Orlando.

73. At Salem, British schooner Diligent, with rum, prize to the privateer Polly.

74. American fisherman, Five Sisters, recaptured by the American privateer Dart.

75. At Portland, British brig Resolution, with flour, peas & cordage, prize to the privateer Nancy.

76. The Privateer Paul Jones, Capt. Hazard of New York, has captured, July 31, off the North side of Porto Rico, the sloop Mary Ann, Capt. T. White of Bermuda, from Turks Island, bound to Antigua, with 3,000 Bushels of salt. The Paul Jones with 3 guns & 160 men sailed July 6th.

77. The brig General Blake, Atkins, under Spanish colours, out 3 days from Amelia, has been sent into Charleston by the revenue Cutter Gallatin, Capt. McNeal.

78. A British ship of 300 tons, from London, bound to Halifax with a cargo consisting of dry goods, crates, glass & Hardware, which cost in England 50,000 Dollars, arrived at Portland, on Monday, taken by the Privateer Teazer of New York. The owner & his wife arrived in the ship. We do not understand whether the owner had insured his property or not.

79. The British schooner Lord Nelson, captured by the United States brig Oneida, on Lake Ontario; she is now cruising in the United States service.

80. New York City, Aug. 19. Arrived here yesterday, and saluted Castle Williams as She passed, the british brig Harmony, from Greenock, bound to Quebeck, with a cargo of rum, dry goods and coal ; captured July 29th, in lat. 46, long. 55, by the privateer Yankee of Bristol, R. I. The Harmony is a fine vessel of 250 tons, mounted 4 sixes, and had 20 men. The Yankee about the same time captured three other brigs, one of which being in ballast was given up for the purpose of getting rid of prisoners.

81. Portland, Aug. 17. Brig Peter Waldo, Charles Warren, master, prize to the privateer Teazer, captured off Halifax, bound from New Castle to Halifax, cargo of Hardware, Powder, &c.

82. Boston, Aug. 22. Arrived ship Eliza Ann, prize to the Yankee Privateer, Sailed 6th July from Liverpool for Baltimore, Sailed in co. with the brig Canon of NewYork, Aug. 3. Lat. 45, Long. 42, fell in with a fleet of 97 sail under convoy of a sloop of War, 29 days from Jamaica for England. The Yankee had taken 7 English vessels.

83. Portland. Arrived schooner John & George of New York, from Lisbon, Wm. Malloy, prize Master, prize to the privateer Regulator, Capt. Mansfield of Salem. The above schooner has on board about 300 boxes of Lemons. Aug. 3d, when east of Cape Sable, The Regulator fell in with her having all sail standing and somewhat torn — when, on boarding her, found that she was entirely deserted and not an article of provisions was left. It appears by her logbook, that she had been captured by the British frigate Africa, and ordered for Halifax, and from the last date of her Journal she had been deserted about 4 days.

84. An English brig laden with Timber arrived at Cape Ann, on Saturday, first captured by a Salem privateer, then recaptured by an English frigate, and afterwards by a Lynn privateer.

85. Boston, Aug. 22. Arrived, British brig William, prize master Chittendon, from Bristol, Eng., prize to the privateer Rossie Barney of Baltimore, taken Aug. 2, Lat. 46.30, Long. 50, has a cargo of 150 tons coal, cheese, butter, pork, &c.

86. Salem, Aug. 21. Arrived, the beautiful British brig Coves, with timber, &c., prize to the John. She is nearly a a new vessel, copper bolted and fastened, 225 tons burthen.

87. Philadelphia, Aug. 21. Arrived at this port Privateer schooner Gov. McKean, Lucet, from a cruise and brought in with her the British Packet Prince Adolphus, Capt. Boulderson (this is the Gentleman who fired upon Washington Morton off the hook), taken the 9th inst. in Lat. 24.48, long. 63.8, bound from Martinico for Falmouth, having 18 guns & 36 men. Had on board the Governor, Paymaster, & Collector of Demerara.

88 to 95 inclusive. An English ship of 450 tons, with coffee, from Martinique for London, has arrived at Baltimore, prize to the privateer Tom of that place.

An English ship from Dublin in ballast, 5 brigs and 1 schooner were burnt by the Rossie, Com. Barney. The Rossie has taken on the present cruise Eleven British vessels.

96 to 98 inclusive. The privateer brig Yankee of Bristol, R. I., was spoken July 6, lat. 44.30, long. 52.43, had captured since she left port the following English vessels; viz., Brig

Alfred, Truman, 2 guns, from Newfoundland, burnt; brig Thetis, of and from Poole with coals, burnt; Ship Royal Bounty (an old vessel of 700 tons), from Hull in ballast, burnt, mounting ten 6-pounders & 20 men.

99, 100. A British ship and 1 schooner, prizes to the Teazer privateer of New York, arrived at Portland, on Monday. The schooner loaded with rum & sugar could not learn the cargo of the ship. The Teazer had also arrived at Portland.

101. Arrived at New York. The schooner Industry, Capt. Clamerna of St. Georges Bay, a prize the privateer Benjamin Franklin, Capt. Ingersol, Captured Aug. 7.

102. Portland, Aug. 10. Arrived at Portland, Barque St. Andrews from Bristol, England, prize to the privateer Rapid, Crabtree, of this port.

103. Salem, Aug. 23. Arrived, British schooner Nancy, with a full cargo of dry fish & provisions, prize to the privateer Fair Trader of this port.

104. The British brig Henry, from Gibraltar, prize the privateer Yankee, has arrived at Newport.

105. Baltimore, Aug. 22. Arrived, British schooner Ann, from City St. Domingo for Guernsy, with mahogany & logwood, sent in by the privateer Globe, Murphy, of this port. The Ann was taken the 14th inst., lat. 29.48, long. 65; mounts 4 guns 9 men.

106. Arrived at Boston, on Thursday last, a large British clump brig, prize to the Benjamin Franklin of New York.

107. The Slyvia of Boston, taken by the British brig Goree, and retaken by the Gov. McKean has arrived at Philadelphia.

108. On the 7th of August, Com. Barney captured the British ship Jenny, Stewart (who has arrived at Salem), from Liverpool for St. John's, N. S., with salt; mounting 12 guns and 18 men.

109. The American brig Adeline, from London, bound to Bath, loaded with dry goods, had been taken by the British brig of War Avenger, and recaptured by the U. S. Frigate Constitution, Capt. Hull.

Brilliant Naval Victory!

110. Boston, Aug. 31, 1812. The United States Frigate Constitution, Capt. Hull, anchored here yesterday in the outer harbour from a short cruise, during which she fell in with the English Frigate Guerriere, which she captured after a short but severe action. The damage sustained by the fire of the Constitution was so great, that it was found impossible to tow her into port, and accordingly the crew were taken out and the ship sunk. The Constitution's loss in the action was 7 men killed and 7 wounded. The Guerriere's was 15 men killed and 64 wounded.

111, 112. The Constitution has also taken and destroyed two English brigs, one in ballast, the other loaded with lumber, bound to England.

113. New York, Aug. 29. Last night, arrived at this port, the British brig Eliza, from Jamaica for England, laden with rum & sugar, prize to the Marengo privateer of this port.

114. Also arrived at New York, a British brig from Quebec for Bermuda, a prize to the Bunker Hill privateer of this port.

115. New York, Aug. 28. The privateer Paul Jones of this port has put into Savannah for provisions and water, and took with her a prize worth $200,000 ; cargo, dry goods and rum.

116. Baltimore, Aug. 25. Arrived, British schooner Harriet (Taylor, prize master), from New Providence for Havannah, in ballast and specie, sent in by the High Flyer privateer; was captured on the 15th inst. off the Doubleheaded shot. On board is a Spanish lady who was a passenger on board the Spanish schr. Antelope from New York for Havannah, which was taken by an English man-of-war.

117. Captured by Com. Rodgers, July 2d, lat. 45, long. 43 ; took the English brig Traveller from Quebeck bound to New Castle, cargo of spars, — burnt.

118. July 4th, lat. 47, long. 30, took the English brig Dutchess from Portland, Capt. Thompson of South Shields, from New Castle bound to Pictou in ballast ; burnt.

119. Arrived at Norfolk, Aug. 24, privateer schooner Globe, Capt. Murphy of Baltimore, from a cruise. She came in with her prize, the ship Sir Simon Clarke, Capt. Udney, of 16

guns and 39 men ; a new ship on her first voyage, 377 tons, bound from Jamaica to Leith, with a cargo of 343 hhds. & 51 tierces of sugar, 91 puncheons of rum, coffee, logwood & mahogany, &c.

Charleston, Aug. 19. The privateer schooner Mary Ann, Capt. Chazal, returned to this port yesterday, after a short cruise of 28 days. On this cruise she has captured 4 prizes, two of which she has brought in with her, one she burnt and the other was given up to the prisoners. The prizes arrived are : —

120. British brig Amelia, Harris, from Malta, bound to Havana with a valuable cargo of oil, wine, soap, cork, wood, &c. She mounts 10 guns but had only 14 men.

121. Also British brig Honduras Packet, Curtis, from Jamaica bound to the City of St. Domingo, with a cargo of provisions, &c. ; mounts 2 guns, with 12 men.

122. The vessel destroyed was a small British schooner loaded with cotton from Gonaives for Jamacai. The prizes were all taken within a short distance of the Island of Jamacai.

123. Arrived at Charleston, Aug. 18. British schooner Perseverance in ballast, prize to the Nonesuch privateer, Capt. Levely, of Baltimore.

124. Arrived at Philadelphia, Ship Superior Bennett, from Liverpool, with a cargo of dry goods and ironmongery to the amount of 250,000 *l*. Sterling, a prize to Gunboat No. 129.

125. Philadelphia, Aug. 31. Last evening arrived in town, the prize master of the ship John, of 16 guns of Lancaster (Eng.), from London for Martinique, arrived at the Lazarette, was taken by the Hornet, one of our squadron, the 27th of July.

126. Arrived at this port (Boston), yesterday, British brig Hazard (late Holiday), of North Shields, 64 days from New Castle, was bound to Shubenancady, N. S., prize to the sloop-of-war Wasp ; 16th of Aug., lat. 44, long. 57, the Hazard was taken by the privateer Dolphin of Salem, retaken Aug. 24th, lat. 41, long. 64, by the Æoulus Frigate, and Finally by the Wasp, Aug. 25th. The Hazard is in ballast, mounts six 12-pound carronades, is copper-bottomed and is 238 tons.

127, 128, 129. Arrived at Newport, on Monday the 31st inst.,

The privateer Rossie, Com. Barney, with a prize, an American ship from Liverpool to New York. On the present cruise, besides what we have taken an account of, she has taken one brig and one schooner sunk.

130. Portsmouth, N. H., Sept. 1. Arrived British schooner Ferebe & Phebe, prize to the Squando of this port.

131. Brig Lady Prevost from Halifax for Jamaica, has arrived at New York, prize to the Marengo privateer. She was taken Aug. 15th.

132. Arrived at New York, British brig Eliza, Sullivan, 48 days from St. Barts, bound to Guernsy with 181 puncheons rum, taken by the Marengo privateer of this port, has 2 guns and 7 men.

133. An English Ship of 300 tons, 8 guns, cargo of salt, crates and iron hoops from Liverpool, arrived at Salem yesterday morning. She was taken to the Eastward of the Grand Banks by the privateer Dromo of this place, and last Sunday by the Montgomery of Salem, the prize master of the Dromo, it is said, not having a copy of her commission.

134. Arrived at Salem an English barque, prize to the privateer Decatur of Newburyport.

135. Arrived at Newport, The fine copper-bottomed British ship Jane of 12 guns, with 20,000 bushels salt. Captured by the privateer Rossie, Com. Barney.

136. The Mary & Susan was sent into this port by the privateer Tickler, Johnson, who took out her letters and papers, and the privateer is at anchor on Staten Island.

137, 138. Two large prize brigs arrived at Portland, on Friday last, taken by the privateer brig Rapid of that place; they were from England bound to St. Andrews in ballast; one of the brigs had 6 guns.

139. The Brig Two Friends of London, with timber, prize to the Benjamin Franklin privateer, was at Hyannis, on Wednesday last. Boston, Sep. 7, 1812.

140. On Friday, Arrived at Salem, the English Ship Gurana, Robert McDowell, late master, from Liverpool, bound to Quebec, prize to the private armed schooner Dromo of Boston, commanded by H. Cooper.

141. St. Mary's, 15th July, 1812. On the evening of the 4th inst., a schooner from Nassau, N. P., ignorant of the war, entered the St. Mary's river bound to Ferdinando with 20,000 Dols. in specie, the property of Logan Lenox & Co. of England, seized by one of the Gun Boat's officers.

142. Also on the 9th inst., A Small schooner from the same place of the former, unapprised of the war, came in with 4 or 5,00 Dols. for the disbursement of an English ship, and 500 dozen pineapples, which was immediately seized.

143, 144, 145. Arrived at Baltimore on the 1st inst., The Highflyer privateer from a cruise, having made four captures.* The british ship Diana, Capt. Harvey, one the fleet from Jamaica bound to Bristol, burthen 350 tons, laden with sugar, rum, coffee, &c. At the same time engaged and took the ship Jamaica of Liverpool, John Neill, master, mounting 7 guns, 21 men, 285 tons burthen, in company with the Ship Mary Ann of London, Miller, master, of 12 guns and 17 or 18 men, 319 tons burthen, also engaged her; the engagement lasted 20 minutes, when we boarded her, she struck at the same time.

An extract of a letter of Sept. 1, confirms the arrival of the above vessels.

146. The Privateer Eagle of New York, mounting 1 gun, has captured the English ship Grenada from Grenada, mounting 9 guns, with 600 hhds. of sugar.

147. Arrived at Norfolk the fine copper-bottomed brig Roebuck, Capt. Kennedy, with 175 hhds. rum, a prize to the schooner Rosamond, Capt. Campam of New York. The Roebuck was bound to Guernsy and captured 5 days after the Rosamond left New York.

148. New York, Aug. 8, 1812. Arrived last evening at Quarantine Ground, the british brig New Liverpool from Minorca for Quebec with a full cargo of wine, prize to the privateer Yankee of Bristol, R. I. This brig is 150 tons burthen, mounts 4 guns and had a crew of 10 men.

149. Baltimore, Sept. 5. The british Ship Hopewell, 400

*The first we have taken down.

tons, from Jamaica for England, with a cargo of sugar & coffee, prize to the Comet privateer, is in sight below.

150. The cargo of the schooner Shaddock, Eutchman, from Antigua, carrying 3 guns, captured by the privateer Eagle, arrived at Charleston, consisted of 39 hhds. & 28 tierces of molasses.

151. British schooner (armed) after a smart brush taken by the Mary Ann & released to discharge her prisoners.

152. Brig Mary, from Scotland for Newfoundland, captured by the Yankee and released to dispose of prisoners 47 in number.

153, 154. One brig & a schooner captured by the Rossie and sent to Newfoundland with the crews of vessels she had taken, 108 in number, on parole & receipt for exchange.

155. Schr. Sally, captured by the Teazer of New York and given up for the purpose of disposing of her prisoners, several of the crews of the prizes entered having sworn to defend the American flag.

156. British brig in ballast, captured by the Polly of Salem, ransomed after taking out a few bales of dry goods.

157. The Privateer Argus has retaken the schooner Victor of Marblehead from the English.

158. A British brig Arrived at Portland on Sunday, said to be coppered and prize to a privateer of that port.

159. Arrived at Salem on Tuesday from a cruise the privateer Dart, Green, having captured on Friday last after considerable resistance the british brig Friends, of 290 tons & 6 guns, with timber, staves, &c. The Friends arrived at Salem yesterday. Boston, Sept. 11, 1812.

160. *Boston Palladium* of Sept. 11th. A Small privateer belonging to Rhode Island (supposed Hiram), arrived at Salem on Wednesay, and brought in with her an English schooner loaded with flour, reported to have been cut out of St. Johns. ☞ It is proved to be the Leader of this port.

161. Newburyport, Sept. 10. Arrived British brig Elizabeth of Liverpool, E., with 75 tons coal and about 85 tons salt, prize to the privateer Decatur of that port.

162. The Privateer Decatur, captured previous to falling in

with the Elizabeth, a brig from Scotland in ballast bound to Newfoundland, and after taking out a few articles and putting on board the crew of the Duke of Savoy, permitted her to proceed.

163. Boston, Sept. 12. Arrived the British brig King George (late Atkinson, master), from Liverpool, prize to the U. S. Frigate Essex, was taken Aug. 7, lat. 45, long. 40, four weeks out, 280 tons, cargo, salt & coals; was bound to St. Johns.

164, 165. The privateer Schooner Atlas, Capt. Moffat, has arrived at Philada' from a successful cruise having captured two valuable ships from the W. Indies, one the Pursuit of London, 450 tons, 16 guns, 18's & 9's, 35 men, the other, the Planter of Bristol, E., with 12-pounders & 15 men ; both with cargoes of sugar, coffee, cotton, cocoa, &c., one has arrived at Baltimore the other at Philadelphia.

166. A large English ship arrived at Gloucester on Saturday, prize to the privateer Montgomery of Salem.

167. Arrived at Portsmouth, 11th inst., privateer schooner Thomas (Capt. Shaw), from a successful cruise. Also british ship Falmouth of Bristol, E., prize to the Thomas, from Jamaica, with a valuable cargo of rum, sugar, coffee, and logwood ; vessel and cargo valued at 200,000 Dols. The Falmouth had 30 men & mounts 14 guns.

168, 169. The small privateer Leader has taken two other small vessels besides the schooner before mentioned, with a load of flour ; they have arrived at Machias.

170. The privateer schooner Mars has captured and sent into Savannah the British brig Leonidas, Capt. Gammock, mounting 10 guns, from Jamaica with a very valuable cargo coffee, sugar, &c., cost about 50,000 Dols. ; the vessel is new and worth 20,000 Dols.

171. Arrived at Portsmouth, N. H., on Thursday, a large British letter of Marque Ship from Jamaica, of 14 guns & 25 men & 435 tons burthen, prize to the privateer Revenge of that port. She is copper-bottomed and has a very valuable cargo, consisting of 449 hhds. sugar, 40 tierces ditto, 144 hhds. rum, 20 tons coffee, 60 tons dyewood.

172, 173, 174. On the 13th of August, lat. 41.04 N., Long. 35.24 W., the frigate Essex, Capt. Porter, captured after an action of about 8 minutes, the English Sloop-of-War Alert, of 18 guns, commanded by Capt. Lougharne. The Essex arrived in the Delaware the 5th inst. Besides other prizes here before mentioned the Essex has taken & burnt 2 English vessels.

175. The British Ship Elizabeth, burthen about 230 tons, loaded principally with sugar, mounting 10 guns and navigated by 21 men, has been sent into Savannah by the privateer Sarah Ann of Baltimore, of 1 gun & 42 men, after smart action ; the prize had 5 men wounded.

176. The British brig Ocean, late Farrish, S. M. Whitlock, prize master, consigned to A. Riker. She was captured Sept. 3d, by the schooner Saratoga, Riker, after an action of 3 quarters of an hour ; carries 7 guns & 21 men, with a cargo of 117 hhds. sugar, 164 puncheons rum, 83 casks coffee, and sundry other articles. She is a new brig, — first voyage.

177. Arrived at Wilmington, N. C., a valuable prize loaded with rum, &c., captured by the privateer Poor Sailor of Charleston.

178. Arrived at Baltimore, British schooner James Trowbridge from Porto Rico for Martinique in ballast, captured on the 20th Aug., off the former port, by the Dolphin of Baltimore.

179. Newport, Sept. 19. Arrived here yesterday, Schooner Two Brothers, Hoyt of Stanford (Conn.), from Bristol (Eng.), laden with tin, iron, copper, &c., bound to Baltimore ; prize to the privateer schooner "United We Stand," of New York. The Two Brothers left Bristol (Eng.), July 12th, and was captured Sept. 10th, off Sandy Hook, by the Acasta, British frigate, and recaptured on Tuesday last by the above-named privateer.

180. The British Ship Quebeck, of the Jamaica fleet, has been captured by the Saratoga privateer. She is at Hurl Gate on her way down the Sound, and her cargo is estimated at 300,000 dols. !

181. A large schooner belonging to Halifax, with a full cargo of rum, from the West Indies, arrived on Saturday last

at Hampton Roads, a prize to the privateer Black Jake of New York, — Mary Ann, her name.

182. The prize Sloop Philadelphia, retaken by the Saratoga, has come down sound loaded with coal & flour from Virginia. The Saratoga privateer is above Hurl Gate. No one hurt on board the Saratoga after an engagement of 75 minutes with the ship Quebec. The Saratoga is full of rum, sugar, coffee & cotton.

183. Arrived at New York, the British Schooner Venus, prize to the Teazer privateer of this port; cargo, rum, sugar & molasses.

184. A British brig, said to be valuable, arrived at Castine on Sunday last, prize to the Dart privateer of Portland.

185 to 188 inclusive. Arrived at Newport, on Wednesday, the privateer brig Decatur, Nichols, from a cruise of 47 days, having captured 11 sail of English vessels, two of which (the Duke of Savoy & Elizabeth) have arrived several days since. Aug. 23d, she took the brig Pomona of 2 guns, from Aberdeen for the river St. Lawrence, and after disarming her sent her to Halifax as a cartel with prisoners; 26th, took brig Devonshire,* loaded with Green fish for St. John's & sent her to france to sell her cargo; brig Concord from do. for do. & Burnt her; brig Hope from Fergumouth for St. John, sent to Halifax as a cartel with prisoners. The Decatur has taken three other valuable vessels which have not arrived. She has not lost a man During her cruise.

189, 190. Salem, Sept. 25th, 1812. Arrived British brig Hannah (170 tons), from Oporto bound to Quebec in ballast, & British sch. Mary from Lisbon bound to Halifax, with some specie, prizes to the privateer Montgomery of this port.

191. A Barque of 400 tons arrived at Marblehead on Saturday evening last, prize to the privateer Decatur; was 21 days from the Isle of Sable, loaded with timber.

192. The Teazer again! A fine British brig nearly new with a cargo of salt, &c., arrived at Portland on Monday afternoon, prize to the privateer Teazer, New York.

*She has arrived at Quimpa, France.

193. Another specimen of Yankee privateering. A British brig arrived at Portland a few days since which was captured by a small whaleboat privateer of that place, and the privateer came into port on the deck of her prize!

194. Arrived at Savannah, schooner Minorca (prize to the privateer Wasp), from Jamaica to Cuba in ballast.

195, 196, 197. Capt. Allen of the privateer schooner Matilda of Philada., arrived at Savannah 18th ult., from a cruise. He has sent into that port the Ship Goelet, present master Lieut. Brown, loaded with salt, crates, steel, porter, coal & pipes for adjudication; also schooner Manager from Jeremie for Turks Island; cargo, coffee, cocoa, corn, &c., ransomed by her captain; also brig Ranger from Cape François for London, of 10 guns & 20 men; cargo, coffee; since arrived at Philadelphia.

198. An English brig with a crago of Fish from Newfoundland for the West Indies, arrived at Cape Ann yesterday, prize to the privateer Thrasher.

199. British ship Commerce, one of the Decatur's prizes, has arrived at Portland; she has on board 450 hhds. sugar, besides other articles. It is said that she was in co. with 2 more of the D.'s prizes, 12 days since.

200. Ship Mariner of London, from Jamaica, with rum & sugar has arrived at Norfolk, prize to the privateer Gov. McKean of Philadelphia.

201, 202, 203, 204. Arrived at Baltimore privateer Dolphin, from a cruise; has made 6 prizes, 3 of which she burnt, two have arrived, and the other a New Providence privateer captured off the Hole in the Wall, has arrived.

205. Arrived at Norfolk British brig Mariana from Jamaica for London, with coffee, logwood, rum, & sugar, prize to the Gov. McKean privateer of Philadelphia. This brig when fallen in with by the privateer was dismasted and entirely deserted, — rigged up jury masts on her and brought her safe into port.

206. Arrived at Portland, British schooner Jennie with rum, sugar, &c., prize to the privateer Teazer, N. Y.

207. An English brig from Teneriffe, cargo of wine, has arrived at New London, prize to the privateer Marengo of New York.

208. Baltimore, Oct. 10. Arrived, the valuable British ship John (late Tyre), Austin prize, master, from Demerara for Liverpool, captured 18th ult., lat. 33, long. 57, after a short action by the privateer Comet, Boyle, of this port. The John is a handsome ship of about 400 tons burthen, mounting 14 guns, 35 men, coppered to the bends; is laden with 742 bales of cotton, 230 hhds. sugar, 105 puncheons rum, 50 casks and 300 bags coffee, a quantity of old copper & Dyewood.

209. A letter from the Captain of the privateer schr. Rapid of Charleston, to his owners, gives the following account of the capture of an English privateer, 20 days after sailing from port : " Saw a sail and concealed the greater part of his men until he got within gunshot; she proved to be an English privateer who commenced firing upon him, which was returned until he got close along side, when he boarded and carried her ; the crew were taken on board and the privateer burnt."

210. The British packet ship Princess Amelia, arrived in Savannah river on Thursday, the 1st inst., a prize to the American Privateer schr. Rossie, commanded by Commodore Barney. The packet mounts 10 guns and had 27 men. She was taken after a desperate engagement of 35 minutes, in which the British Captain, Sailing Master and four men were killed and 6 or 7 wounded. The Rossa had no men killed & but few wounded.

211. The British sch. Woodburn from Havana for Honduras, has arrived at New Orleans, prize to the privateer Brothers of N. O. & Matilda of Philadelphia.

212. British schooner Adella, Smith prize master, from Martinique, with a full cargo of sugars, captured on the 17th Sept., in the sight of Martinique, by the privateer schr. Rosamond of this port. New York, Oct. 17.

213. The privateer Marengo has arrived at New York ; on the present cruise she has taken the British brig Lord Sheffield, from Teneriffe bound to Quebec ; took possession of her but not judging her worth sending in, took out of her 2 pipes of Maderia wine and some provisions — set fire to her and abandoned her about 11 Leagues from Palma.

214, 215. British Ship Favorite, Bryass, of Liverpool, from

Cork, ballasted with grindstones and whetstones, copper bottomed, of about 250 tons, and british brig Sir John Moore, Watson, of and from Dublin, with 6 puncheons rum, 82 chains & a quantity of Sand ballast, have arrived at Lynn, both prizes to the privateer Industry, Mudge, of that place.

216. A schooner, prize to the Fame privateer, arrived at Provincetown, on Sunday last. She is about 155 tons burthen, is from the West Indies, loaded with sugar, and was taken in sight of Halifax harbour.

217. Newport, Oct. 22d, 1812. Yesterday arrived in this harbour, British brig Orient, cargo, timber, &c., prize to the privateer Teazer of New York.

218, 219. The British sch. Caledonia, and brig Adams, taken by our brave sailors who went from Buffalo, on the 8th inst. and cut them out from under the guns of the British Fort Erie, had on board 500,000 Dollars worth of furs belonging to the N. West Company. The sch. was brought into Black Rock harbour, and the Brig Adams was burnt in consequence of her getting aground.

220. An American Privateer has captured a schooner (unknown) from Bay Chalseur, with Salmon & Peltry.*

221. The British schooner Four Brothers, prize to the privateer Fame, arrived at Salem. The F. B. was built in Salem, 6 years since, but was taken by the English some time since.

222. British schooner Single Cap, prize to the Matilda privateer of Philadelphia, has arrived in the Mississippi.

223. British brig Henry, prize to the John privateer, arrived at Salem Friday morning from Liverpool; cargo, salt, coals and crates.

224. The Privateer John, Crowninshield, has recaptured the privateer Industry, Mudge, of Salem, having been risen upon and captured by the prisoners on board:

225. Baltimore, Oct. 20. Arrived British Brig Pointshares, from St. Johns, N. S., for Barbadoes with fish, captured 16th Sep. by the Letter of Marque sch. Baltimore, Veazey, on her way to france.

*British schooner Betsy Ann; she was taken by the Fame.

226. Arrived at Philadelphia Spanish Brig San Antonio from Guernsey, prize to the Marengo of New York, captured on suspicion of her being British property.

227, 228. The British brig Jane from Greenock for Pictou, prize to the Dart of Portland. Also a large schooner with live stock Arrived at Portland, do.

229. Arrived at Savannah on Saturday British schooner Fame, Smith, prize master; dry goods, oil, &c., prize to the privateer sch. Nonesuch, taken Going from Trinadad to Cayenne.

230. The privateer America has captured British sch. Intrepid, and after taking out various articles of her cargo, released her.

231. Arrived at Charleston, British sch. Antelope of Carracas, I. S. Henshaw, prize Master, captured by the Privateer Rosamond of New York ; cargo, dry goods, flour, butter, cheese, hams, &c. The Antelope was formerly a French privateer called the Bonaparte.

232, 233. British brig Neptune of Leith from St. John, N. B., whence she sailed 16th inst. in a fleet of 9 sail convoyed by the brig Plumper, with a cargo of timber, arrived at Salem yesterday, prize to the ship John Privateer of that place. Also arrived there on Sunday evening, British brig Diamond, Lightly, from St. Salvador, bound to England with a cargo of cotton (180,000 lbs.) and logwood, prize to the privateer ship Alfred, of that place.

234. British ship Phenix, carrying 12 nines and sixes, and had 17 men, late Ross, commander, prize to the privateer Mary Ann of Charleston, from Bermuda, bound to Kingston, Jam. ; cargo, 100 pipes Fayal Wine.

235, 236, 237. Also on the present cruise the Mary Ann has destroyed a british cutter loaded with coffee. Yesterday morning, about 20 miles Southward of the bar, fell in with and recaptured the sch. Union. Barker, from this port for New Haven And the sloop Mary Ann for New York, they had both been captured by British men-of-war off that port.

238. Arrived at Savannah, British schooner Dawson, prize to the privateer Wasp, Taylor, of Baltimore. The Dawson's cargo is sugar, coffee, rum, &c.

239. The English brig Industry of London, mounts 10 carriage guns & 20 men, prize to the privateer Comet of Baltimore, arrived at Beaufort, S. C., the 10th inst. Her cargo, 200 bales cotton, 190 hhds. sugar, 40 do. coffee, 80 hhds. molassess, 2 pipes wine, and cocoa, &c.

240. A British brig, with a cargo of salt, coals and crates, prize to the privateer ship America of Salem, arrived at Portsmouth, N. H.

241. The British ship Jane, of Glasgow, from St. Johns with a cargo of Lumber and naval stores, arrived at Salem on Saturday, a prize to the privateer Ship John.

242. British sloop Louisa Ann, Golden, prize master, 20 days from Trinity, Martinique, with 80 hhds. molasses, a prize to the privateer Benj. Franklin, Capt. Ingersoll, of New York, has arrived at that port. The Louisa Ann was cut out of Trinity about the 10th of Oct., at 9 o'clock in the evening by a boat & 7 men from the Benj. Franklin from under a battery of 12 guns, 11-pounders.

243. British brig Industry, prize to the Comet of Baltimore, has arrived at Raleigh, N. C., supposed to be worth 80,000 Dols., bound to London. The cargo consists of 185 hhds. sugar, 20 do. molasses, 104 bales cotton, 10 casks of coffee, 184 bags do., 100 bags cocoa, 8 pipes & 2 hhds. M. Wine.

244, 245. Arrived at Salem, British Ship Ned, mounting 10 guns, copper-bottomed, with timber her cargo, prize to the Revenge. Same day arrived British sch. ———, captured in the Bay of Fundy with a cargo of oil, seal skins, plaister, &c., prize to the Fame, Capt. Green.

246. The English sch. Robbin, taken by the Revenge of Salem, has arrived. Portland.

247. The English schooner Sea Flower, Crosby, of and from Yarmouth, N. S., for St. Andrews, arrived at Salem, on Friday last, prize to the Fame privateer, Capt. Green, taken Oct. 31, near her port of destiny. Cargo, plaister, oil, seal skins, and Salmon.

248. A British armed brig* from the bay of Honduras for

*Brig Francis Blake with a cargo of 49 cattle.

Jamaica was sent into Charleston on the 31st ult., a prize to the Nonsuch privateer of Baltimore.

249. A schooner laden with timber taken by the Saucy Jack of Charleston, and given up to release the prisoners she had made.

250. The privateer Saucy Jack has returned to Charleston after a cruise of 50 days, during which she took seven prizes. Among other truly impudent things the Saucy Jack did, was to enter the harbour of Demara, and by good management, make an easy prize of the very valuable British brig Wm. Rathbone of Liverpool, from London, laden with dry goods worth 40,000 *l.* sterling (just arrived) ; mounting fourteen 18-pounders and two 6's.

251. The Piscataqua, Rogers, from Baltimore for Lisbon, was captured by a British Frigate and ordered for Barbadoes; was recaptured by an American privateer and ordered for Baltimore, and in going up the bay struck on Tangier Bar and Bilged ; she had 3,500 bbls. flour, which will be principally saved.

252. Georgetown, S. C., Oct. 28th. Arrived, privateer sch. Two Brothers, of New Orleans, from a cruise Sept. 26th. Burnt the British sloop Venus in ballast, bound to Jamaica.

253. Arrived at Charleston British sloop ———— of Tortola, in ballast, prize to the privateer Saucy Jack.

254. Arrived at Hampton Roads, the brig Paugy, prize to the privateer High Flyer of Baltimore, laden with rum & molasses from Antigua for Newfoundland.

255. Arrived at Baltimore British packet brig Swallow, of 18 guns, from Jamaica for Falmouth, with the mail and from 150 to 200,000 Dols. in specie, sent in by Commodore Rodgers's Squadron.

256. The English schooner Three Sisters, late Card, one of the Fame's prizes has arrived at Salem. She was from Windsor for St. Andrews loaded with plaister, and is 120 tons burthen.

257. Arrived at Charleston British schooner Sally of Curracoe, from Jamaica, bound to Curracoe, in ballast; captured on the 13th ult. off the bay of Sabines by the privateers Black Jake & G. Washington.

258. Arrived at Philada. British brig St. Antonio, Kenedy, prize master, prize to the privateer Marengo of New York.

259. Arrived at Charleston, the British Brig John, a prize to the privateer Benjamin Franklin of this port,* with a valuable cargo and 40,000 Dols. in specie.

260, 261. The British Schooner Mary Hatt, and sloop Elizabeth (merchant vessels) arrived at Sacket's Harbour, prize to the squadron under Commodore Chauncy, on Lake Ontario, having been captured bound from York to Kingston.

262, 263, 264. Arrived British schooner Comet, of 2 guns and small arms complete, Tinkham, prize master, taken off the south side of St. Domingo by the privateer Rapid of Charleston. She is loaded with sugar, beeswax, tobacco & dry goods. The Rapid took, and burnt off Abaco, a New Providence privateer, Searcher, of 1 gun and 20 men. Also captured schooner Mary (British), but ransomed her on account of not having men to spare to send her in.

265. The British brig Union (late Sharp), from Guernsey for Grenada, in ballast, arrived at Old Town on Friday. She was captured Oct. 26, by the schooner privateer Gen. Armstrong, Barnard, from New York.

266. The schooner Favorite of Ellsworth, with 114 bbls. flour and 7,000 bushels corn, from Virginia, captured off Cape Cod by the Eng. privateer Liv. Packet, was recaptured off Cape Sable by the privateer Revenge of Salem and arrived at Cape Ann on Saturday morning.

267. Arrived at Portland, the British Barque Fisher from Rio Janeiro for London, laden with a valuable cargo of hides, Tallow, cotton & specie & a few Boxes of chrystal stones for Jewelry. She was taken 55 days since off the Western Islands by the privateer Fox of Portsmouth.

268. British schooner taken & destroyed by Com. Chauncy on Lake Ontario.

269. English ship Freedom of Pool, from Cadiz, with 700 hhds. salt bound to St. Johns, arrived at Marblehead, prize to the Thorn privateer. She is a handsome ship, 3 years old, and mounting 6 guns.

*New York.

ANOTHER NAVAL VICTORY!!

Hall, Decatur & Jones forever !

270. Capture of the BRITISH Frigate Macedonian. She was captured on the 20th of October, in Lat. 30, Long. 26, By the United States frigate United States, Commodore Decatur, *after an action of 17 minutes.* THERE WERE 104 MEN KILLED AND WOUNDED on board the Macedonian & 12 (only) on board the United States. The Macedonian arrived at Newport, R. I., Dec. 6th, 1812.

271. The British brig Lady Harriet, from Cadiz, in ballast, a prize to the privateer Orders in Council, Capt. Howard of ———, has arrived at the Hook. She was cut out of Turks Island.

272 to 275 inclusive. A large copper-bottomed English Brig from England, in ballast, bound to Jamaica, arrived at New London, 4th inst., prize to the Joel Barlow privateer of New York. Arrived at New York the privateer Orders in Council from a cruise of 12 weeks from off Barbadoes, St. Domingo, &c. She has made 5 prizes, 3 of which she ransomed and 2 manned and ordered for the U. States.

276. Arrived at Salem British brig Bacchus of and from port Glasgow, 15 weeks, in ballast, and 29 passengers, men, women and children, prize to the privateer Revenge of Salem.

277. British sloop Nelly, with a cargo sugar, coffee, rum, &c., captured about four weeks since by the Revenge privateer, has been driven ashore on Chincoteague shoals—a good prize.

278. The British Brig Venus, prize to the Polly of Salem, arrived at Savannah 30th ult.

279. The British schooner Louen, from Martinico for St. Martins, with coffee and sugar, arrived at Cape May 7th inst., prize to the Revenge of Philadelphia.

280. Arrived at Norfolk, A British South sea ship with 1,400 casks of oil and 15 tons of ebony, a prize to the Frigate Congress, Capt. Smith.

281. Arrived at Boston schooner Sally, Cousins, with salt, prize to the Dromo of that place ; she was taken out of Cape Split.

282. The privateer Joel Barlow has retaken the sch. Signora Del Carmel, and after taking out 3 trunks, 1 chest, and 1 tierce dry goods, 1 trunk cigars and a hhd. Glassware, and a few pieces of cotton released her.

"Bon Prizes."

283, 284. The British sch. Neptune with a cargo of salt, oil & fish, prize to the Revenge of Salem was cast away below Portland on her passage to Salem. Part of her cargo, sails, rigging, &c., saved. The Revenge on her present cruise has driven an english schooner ashore on the coast of N. Scotia, and burnt her.

285 to 294 inclusive. Arrived in Chesapeake Bay the British ship John Hamilton, from Honduras for London, with 700 tons mahogany, is a large ship, 120 feet on deck, captured the 25th ult., after a long action without the loss of any lives ; the ship mounts 4 long 9's and 12-pound carronades and 30 men. By the Dolphin privateer of Baltimore. The privateer schooner Patriot, Merrihew of New York, has arrived at George Town, S. C., after a cruise of 56 days, during which she burnt, sunk & destroyed nine British vessels.

295. Schooner John Bull, a King's Packet, cut out of New Providence, chased on shore on Crooked Island By the Rover of New York.

296, 297. Arrived at New York, from a cruise of 10 weeks, the privateer Gen. Armstrong. On the 31st of Oct., off Cousanter River, Dutch guana, captured the sch. Tyger of Berbia bound to Surrinam. Not being of much value gave her up with the brig Union's crew (a prize taken previous). On the 25th off Demerara, captured the sch. Fame from Barbadoes bound to Demerara ; not being worth sending in liberated her.

298. Arrived at New York, sloop Caroline, Evelith, prize master, from Quebeck, bound to Tortula ; cargo, flour & staves, captured by the Retaliation privateer of that port.

299. Arrived at New York British brig two Friends, prize to the privateer Benj. Franklin.

300. Arrived at Baltimore privateer sch. Bona from a cruise.

She has taken (besides other prizes not arrived) the British Packet Townsend, Capt. Coy, from Falmouth for Barbadoes, she picked up in the ocean, the mail which she had thrown overboard, and brought it safe into port. The packet was ransomed and proceeded on her voyage.

301. Letter of marque brig Leo Libby, sailed from Portland some time since for France, has captured the British brig Pomona, coppered to the bends & mounting six 12-pounders, bound from Lisbon to Newfoundland, has arrived at Belfast, Maine.

302. A Schooner, Dolphin, prize to Liverpool packet, has been retaken by the Americans on board, and arrived at North Yarmouth, Maine.

303, 304. Arrived at Baltimore, British schooner Barchal, Lightburn, from Barbadoes, in ballast, sent in by the High Flyer. The high flyer had taken a number of drogers plying between the islands, which she released ; one of them she sent into Demerara, as a flag of truce, with the commissary and 72 prisoners she had on board. ☞ See particulars.

305. Arrived at Charleston, S. C., privateer schooner Revenge, from a cruise ; mounts 14 guns. Besides number of other prizes not proper to mention here, captured the British schooner Neptune, but gave her up to dispose of her prisoners.

306. Arrived at Charleston, S. C., a British ship, prize to the Highflyer privateer.

307. Arrived at Salem, British brig Dart of Port Glasgow, from Grenada for Glasgow with a cargo of 65 hhds. of rum, 155 bales of cotton and 400 scroons of do., and some other articles, prize to the privateer ship America of Salem.

308. Arrived at Wilmington, British ship Betsy from Glascow, prize to the privateer revenge of Baltimore, with 20,000 Dols. in specie on board, which was taken on board the privateer.

309. British Ship Queen captured by the General Armsrong privateer, on her passage to New York, was cast away on Nantucket shoals. She was valued at 100,000 *l*. sterling.

310. Arrived at Charleston, S. C., privateer Tom of Balti-

more, of 14 guns & 117 men. The Tom has captured a British packet from London bound to Barbadoes harbour, and in sight of some hundreds of the inhabitants. The British packet has been ransomed by her captain.

311. The British brig Recovery from Quebeck for Jamaica, cargo pickled fish, staves & lumber, prize to the U. S. Brig Argus, has arrived at Holmes Hole.

312. Arrived at Savannah, a Bermudian-built schooner, copper-bottomed, loaded with dry goods and Irish butter. She was bound from Jamaica to Spanish Main ; prize to the privateer Liberty of Baltimore, of 1 gun & 40 men.

313, 314, 315. Arrived at New London, privateer Jack's Favorite of New York, from a cruise of 4 months, during which she captured 7 vessels, 3 of which were destroyed.

316. Arrived at Salem, Schooner Lucy with a cargo of salt, rum, hardware, &c. She was originally bound from Plymouth to the southward ; was captured off the Capes by the British sloop-of-war Sylph, and recaptured by the Montgomery privateer.

317, 318, 319. The British Ship Ralph, and brig Eupheria, two of the privateer America's prizes, arrived at Portland on Saturday, and the ship Hope taken by Ditto, arrived at Marblehead on Sunday. Boston, Jan'y 27th, 1813.

320. British brig Lucy & Mida, from London for Surrinam, with a cargo of dry goods, has arrived at Norfolk, prize to the privateer revenge.

321. Arrived at New London, schooner Rebeccah of Halifax, prize to the privateer Jack's Favorite.

322, 323, 324. Arrived at New London, British ship Rio-Nova of London, about 450 tons, prize to the privateer Rolla of Baltimore ; her cargo is said to be worth 40,000 *l.* sterling. She had 18 guns & 30 men ; the Rolla also captured schooner brisk of London, of 2 guns & burnt her ; and schooner Barbara of 4 guns & gave her to the prisoners.

325. Brig Ohio from Philadelphia, laden with flour & corn, arrived below Portsmouth on Sunday. She had been captured by the British and after being in their possession for 18 days was retaken by the privateer Fox.

326. Arrived at Newport, British Ship Mary from Bristol (Eng.), bound to Maderia. The Mary was captured Dec. 11th, 1812, by the privateer Rolla of Baltimore ; the ship mounts 10 guns, is coppered to the bends, having an assorted cargo of iron, salt, porter, cider, coals, &c.

327, 328. Arrived at Savannah, the privateer schooner Liberty, after a cruise of 3 months, Nov. 23d, being off Cape Delaware, took the sch. Maria from Jamaica bound to the bay of honduras, having nothing but ballast, ransomed her for 600 Dols. Nov. 25th, captured the schooner William, Capt. Roach, from Kingston (Jam.), bound to Porto Cavello, put a prize master & ten men on board and ordered her to Savannah, where she has arrived.

329. The Walter, Whitney, of Philadelphia, was captured by a british brig on her passage from St. Iago to New Orleans ; a prize master & 17 men put on board and ordered for Nassau (N. P.), Capt. Whitney & two boys being left on board, retook the ship & have carried her into Savannah.

330. Arrived at Boston British brig Peggy of St. Johns (N. F.), with fish & oil, bound to Barbadoes, prize to the privateer Hunter.

331. The schooner Juliana Smith of Philadelphia, with a cargo of coffee, captured by the Maidstone off the southern coast, and recaptured by the Montgomery, has arrived at Cape Ann.

332. The British brig Barrassa, prize to the Rolla of Baltimore, arrived at Tarpaulin cove on Wednesday last ; cargo, dry goods, Tallow, &c.

333. A British Ship of 500 tons, mounting 8 guns, with a cargo of coal, bricks, and plantation utensils, from Bristol (Eng.), bound to the W. Indies, has arrived at New London, prize to the Growler of Salem, privateer.

Good ! Good !!

334. Arrived at Port Penn, the Lady Johnson, an ordnance transport from London, prize to the privateer Comet, laden with 40 pieces battering cannon, a large quantity of Congreve rockets, 2,000 barrels of Gunpowder (90 lbs. in each cask), a

number of musketry & accoutrements in boxes, cordage in abundance & variety of other articles consisting of munitions of war. The Lady Johnson sailed from London for Quebeck with the above valuable cargo for the supply of the British armies in Canada.

335. Arrived at Charleston, privateer sch. Eagle, from a cruise; Decr. 24th captured schooner Maria, under Spanish Colours, with British property on board, from Jamaica for St. Domingo City ; took out her cargo of dry goods and let her go, after putting on board all the prisoners.

336. Arrived at Charleston British schooner Erin from Curraca bound to Jamaica with a cargo of dry goods, prize to the private armed schooner Eagle, Capt. Condy, of the former place.

337, 338. Arrived in Savannah River on the 30th of Jan'y, the prize Brig Andalusia, Whimpenry, of 10 guns, captured after an action of 2 hours and a half by the privateer Yankee of Bristol, R. I. The Andalusia was captured on the coast of Africa, had 10 guns, 90 negroes, slaves— & 20 whites. The Yankee has taken a sloop, took out of her 452 oz. of gold dust, 5 tons of ivory and sundry bales of goods and gave her up to dispose of the prisoners.

339, 340. A British brig and schooner, captured by the privateer Decatur, off Madeira, and sent to France.

341. Schooner Meadow, captured by the Sparrow of Baltimore and released after divesting her of a quantity of dry goods.

342. The privateer Gallinipper of 2 guns has arrived at Marblehead from a cruise. Has taken only one schooner which she ransomed.

343. Schooner Helen, from London for St. Salvador, captured by the U. S. Sloop-of-war Hornet, off the latter port, the cargo of her put on board the *Constitution* and vessel given up.*

344. The British schooner Nova, taken by the U. S. Frigate Essex, with 70,000 Dols. in specie, which was taken on board of the Essex, and the prize ordered for the United States.

*She was not given up but has arrived at the Southward.

February 17th, 1813.

ANOTHER SPLENDID NAVAL VICTORY OVER THE ENEMY.

345. On Monday evening arrived in the outer harbour (Boston) the United States Frigate CONSTITUTION, Com. Bainbridge. On the 29th Dec., lat. 13.6 S., long. 38 W., about 10 leagues from the coast of Brazils, the CONSTITUTION fell in with and captured His B. Majesty's Frigate JAVA of 49 guns, & manned with upwards of 400 men. The action continued one hour and Fifty minutes, in which time the JAVA *was made a complete wreck, having her bowsprit, and every mast & spar shot out of her.* For particulars see "War."

$100,000.

346. A large, coppered English brig, arrived at Portland on Monday, a prize to the privateer brig Decatur of Newburyport. Her cargo is brandy, wines, dry goods, &c.

$150,000.
$200,000.

347, 348. British ship Volunteer of 400 tons, with a cargo of dry goods and copper, has arrived at Portsmouth, N. H., a prize to the U. St. Frigate CHESAPEAKE, and brings advices that the chesapeake had captured another prize, which she had burnt after taking out of her goods to the amount of 200,000 Dols.

349. Privateer Growler, Graves, of Salem, from a cruise, has arrived at Holmes Hole. Besides, the ship arrived at New London, she has taken the schooner Prince of Wales, and after taking out a few pipes Maderia Wine released her.

$350,000.

350 inclusive 354. The British ship Aurora of and from Liverpool for Pernambuco, with a valuable cargo of dry goods, &c. (the ship is nearly 600 tons, and cargo valued at *350,000 dols.*), has arrived at Newport, prize to the privateer Holkar of New York.

Arrived at New London, privateer Mars from a cruise of 100 days, during which she took 11 prizes, only one has yet arrived, Sloop ———, Sydleman, with a cargo of fruit; she destroyed one & dispatched two for England with prisoners on parole.

355. Arrived at New Orleans, an English ship mounting 20 guns, a prize to the privateer Spry, with a cargo of mahogany & Logwood.

$100,000.

356. Arrived at Marblehead, the British brig Ann, from Liverpool bound to N. Providence with a cargo of dry goods and crates valued at 80 or 100,000 Dols., prize to the privateer Growler of Salem.

357, 358. Arrived at Newport British transport ship Lord Keith, prize to the privateer Mars of New London; mounts 4 guns. Also arrived at Newport, His Brittanick M. brig Emu, of 10 guns, prize to the privateer Holkar of New York, with 86 bales & packages of dry goods.

359. Arrived at Charleston, British brig Pelican, captured on the 23d Decr., off cape St. Vincent, by the privateer Mars of New London.

360. British schoooner George, cut out of Tradestown, cargo rice, part taken out and vessel given up to the prisoners. She was taken by the Yankee.

361. Arrived at Boston, British brig Harriot & Matilda, from Liverpool for Pernambuco, captured off the latter port, 31st Jan'y, by the privateer Yankee of Bristol, R. I. She is 262 tons, mounts 8 guns, 12 & 18 pound carronades & has an assorted cargo of salt, crates, iron, butter, cheese, dry goods, &c. Her dry goods were taken on board the privateer.

362. The privateer Lovely Lass arrived at New Orleans on the 23d Feb., with a prize schooner said to be worth $10,000.

363. A large British Barque arrived at St. Mary's, prize to the privateer Hazard of Charleston, laden with rum, sugar, coffee, &c., from Dominique, bound to London.

364, 365. Arrived at New York privateer Paul Jones, from a cruise of 3 months; besides 7 other prizes not arrived, she has taken British Transport Ship Canada, mounting 10 guns, having 100 troops on board & 42 horses, disarmed the troops & ransomed the ship for 3,000 *l.* sterling; also captured the brig John & Isabella of Berwick or Tweed; being short of provisions, gave her up to the prisoners.

366, 367, 368. Arrived at Bristol, British brig Shannon, from Maranham, bound to Liverpool ; carriage guns, 9's & 6's, 15 men ; 210 tons burthen, with a full cargo of cotton (100 tons), captured on the 24th Feb., 1813, after an action of ten minutes. Vessel & cargo valued at 50,000 Dols.

A RECAPTURE.—A gentleman from Eric states, that Capt. Daniel Dobbin, Naval officer of that place, has recently discovered the Salina (the vessel he lost at Detriot when Hull capitulated), ice bound about 10 miles from Eric ; she was loaded with provisions, munitions of war, &c. Another vessel has been discovered in that quarter in a similar condition, said to be the Chippewa, owned by Mr. Alexander of Fort Erie, being driven out by the wind and being surrounded by the ice they were abandoned.

369. A sloop loaded with hides, prize to a North Carolina privateer, arrived at Newbern, Feb. 24th. She brought in a bundle of dispatches intercepted on their way to the Spanish Government, which have been sent to Washington.

370. The privateers *United we stand & Divided we fall*, of New York, have sent a British brig into Savannah with a valuable carge of dry goods. The prize is copper-bottomed, and armed with 10 guns.

371. March 18th, 1813. Arrived at New York, British brig Three Brothers, from Liverpool, captured by the privateer dolphin, Stafford, of Baltimore. This brig was from Malta for Liverpool, with a full cargo of sumach, sulphur, oil, tallow, corkwood, cotton, acorns & nutgalls.

FIFTH NAVAL VICTORY.

A Brilliant Victory.

372. On the 25th of Feb., 1813, the U. N. S. sloop-of-War, Hornet, fell in with his B. Majesty's brig *Peacock*, Capt. Peake, of 19 guns & 134 men, which he sunk after a close action of 15 minutes ; she unfortunately sunk carrying down 19 of her crew, & (as Capt. Lawrence says) 3 of my brave fellows. For particulars see War.

373. A British brig, prize to the Paul Jones of New York, has arrived at Chatham ; she was destitute of provisions.

374. The British brig Antrini, prize to the privateer Saucy Jack of Charleston, has arrived at New Orleans.

375. The British brig Fly, prize to the Yankee of Bristol, has arrived at Charleston, S. C., said to be valuable.

376. The British ship Robert Nelson, of 600 tons, taken out of the Cork fleet, for the West Indies, with an assorted cargo for the plantations, has arrived at New Orleans, prize to the Saratoga privateer of New York, — Come to an excellent market.

ANOTHER NAVAL ENGAGEMENT.

377. The United States schooner Adeline, engaged in Chesapeake Bay the British schooner Lottery, and after a smart action she made off, but sunk before she got the fleet.

378. Arrived at Portsmouth, N. H., privateer Fox, from a cruise ; her only prizes, the brig Ohio, arrived anterior to her, and a British schooner, which was ransomed.

379. A New Providence privateer was captured by the privater Hazard, but the captain of the Hazard was obliged to abandon her for the sake of getting in another prize which he had previously taken.

380. The huge ship Neptune, sent into New Orleans by the privateer Saratoga, privateer of N. York.

381. The United States Sloop of War Hornet, captured 'on the 4th of Feb., off Pernambuco, the English brig Resolution, of 10 guns, from Rio Janerio for Marohan with jerk beef, flour, &c., and 23,000 Dols. in specie ; took out the money & burnt the brig, not having spare men enough to man her & she being a dull sailer.

382. The British brig Earl Percy, prize to the Frigate Chesapeake is ashore on Long Island ; she is dismasted and has bilged and her cargo of salt all lost. The brig will be got off.

383. Arrived at Savannah, schooner Hussar, a prize to the privateer schooner Liberty of Baltimore, taken off Nassau and bound to Bermuda with turtle, yams, sheep, &c., supposed to be provisions for Admiral Warren, — *a present.*

384. British ship Mentor, prize to the Saucy Jack, has arrived at New Orleans ; a very valuable prize.

385. British ship Albion, 12 guns, 25 men, from Demerara for London with a cargo of 400 hhds. of sugar, 69 puncheons

rum, 10 bales of cotton, 300 bags & 36 casks of coffee, sent into St. Marys by the privateer Hazard, of 3 guns.

386. Arrived at Bristol, British letter of marque schooner Alder, 6 guns, prize to the Yankee of Bristol, R. I. ; cargo, gunpowder (400 casks), muskets, flints, bar lead and iron, dry goods, &c. The Alder is coppered and was formerly a french privateer.

387. Arrived at Newport, Sloop Yankee of Nantucket, Capt. Hussey. The Yankee was cut out of Holmes Hole the day previous of her arrival at Newport by a british fishing smack, but the captain rose upon the crew and betook her.

388. The privateer Thrasher has captured the British schooner Good Intent, from Newfoundland for Portugal with dry fish, and ordered her for France.

389. Arrived at Marblehead, British brig Rover from Jamaica for St. Johns; has a cargo of 184 puncheons of rum, prize to the privateer Alfred of Salem.

390. The privateer Globe of Baltimore fell in with the British ship Seaton dismasted, a prize to the Paul Jones of New York, took out the crew and burnt the Seaton.

391. The brig Criterion of New York was captured by a british frigate and recaptured by the Letter of marque ship Volant & since arrived at Passage, France.

392. Brig Return of London, from Cumana, in ballast, has arrived at Chatham, prize to the Paul Jones.

393. British brig Thomas of and for Liverpool, Eng., from Mayomba (coast of Africa), captured 10th Jan'y, off Anabono', by the privateer brig Yankee of Bristol, R. I. ; she mounts 8 gus and has a cargo 250 tons of redwood, and some other articles were taken out of her and put on board the Yankee.

394, 395. The letter of marque schooner Vesta of Baltimore, on her outward passage to France, fell in with a convoy of transports from Lisbon for England, captured one of the transports & a cutter and burnt them in sight of the fleet.

396. Schooner Albert of Baltimore, taken by the Chesapeake squadron and recaptured by the America of Baltimore, has arrived at Newbern.

397. Arrived at Boston, schooner Valeria, recaptured by the United States Frigate Chesapeake.

398. Ashore at Nantucket, London Packet Thompson, prize to the Paul Jones privateer, in ballast.

399. New London, April 16th. On Wednesday, the smack Hero of Mystic, with a number of volunteers under the command of Capt. Burrows, sailed in pursuit of the Fox which has annoyed our coasters so much. She decoyed her so near that she was unable to escape. The Hero ran her on board when no opposition was made. The Fox was brought into Mystic and this evening her crew were brought up here consisting of a Lieut., midshipman and 11 men. The Fox was captured within ten miles of Block Island.

400 inclusive 405. Savannah, April 11th. This day was brought in the celebrated picaroon Caledonia, captured the day before by the U. S. Schooner Nonsuch, Lieut. Mork.

Arrived at Charleston, S. C., private armed schr. Divided We fall, from a cruise of 108 days, in company with the United We stand, in [which they captured 7 prizes, two of which they ransomed, 2 given up and one sunk.

406 to 412 inclusive. The vessels captured on the Spanish Main by the Snap Dragon privateer of Newbern (N. C.), divested of their valuables and burnt. Three others taken by the same, valuable articles removed and given up to release the prisoners. Sloop ———, a fine coppered-bottomed vessel taken by the Snap Dragon and fitted out as a tender and store ship.

413. An English brig from the Brazils bound home arrived at Salem on Monday the 10th, prize to the privateer ship Alexander, Capt. Crowninshield ; she was captured about 26 days since and has a cargo of 180 tons cotton, &c.

414, 415. An English Frigate of 32 guns and the Duke of Gloucester of 8 guns taken & the former destroyed upon the approval of the U. S. army at Little York, U. C. (See official account.)

416. British Frigate Tartar, prize to the Gen. Armstrong of Charleston, was chased ashore near Georgetown, S. C., and bilged. The cargo, 100 puncheons of rum, was saved.

417. The privateer schooner Fox from Wiscassett, arrived at Portsmouth on Wednesday, with an English brig from Jamaica, with rum, &c., which she captured off that port the day before.

418, 419. Arrived at Savannah, british privateer schooner

Richard, captured off Anguilla, prize to the privateer brig Holkar of New York. The same day captured the privateer sloop Dorcas, gave her up to the prisoners after destroying her of her armament.

420. The english privateer Crown, of 1 large gun and about 20 men was captured off Waldoboro' by a sloop fitted out at that place manned with about 20 Volunteers and commanded by Capt. Tucker, an old naval officer.

421. The english brig Malvina, of ten guns, with a cargo of wine & cork, has arrived at Ocracock, N. C., taken by the letter of marque schooner Ned of Baltimore.

422. A British schooner from Bermuda for Halifax, with wheat, corn, silks, &c., prize to the privateer boat Fame, of Salem, has arrived at Salem, or Machias.

423. Ship sent into Brest (France) by the privateer "True Blooded Yankee," said to be worth from 4 to 500,000 Dols.

424. Brig Charlotte with a cargo of dye woods, &c., was captured in the *english channel* by the privateer Montgomery of Salem and sent into that port.

425. Arrived at Providence, R. I., British ship Nancy, of 300 tons, from Madeira with a cargo of salt, wine and fruits, prize to the privateer Yorktown of New York.

426. Arrived at Boston british packet ship May-Ann, from Malta, bound to Falmouth, prize to the privateer Gen. Armstrong of New York, captured off Cape St. Vincent after an engagement of about one hour. The May-Ann mounts ten guns and had 38 men. She is a fine ship, coppered to the bends, and is about 240 tons burthen.

427. Ship Sabine on her passage from Baltimore for France captured a british brig from Lisbon for London, with a cargo of cotton, and burnt her.

428 to 431 inclusive. Arrived at Portland, privateer Invincible Napoleon, prize to the young Teazer of New York. The I. N. was formerly a French privateer & taken by the British brig of war Atutine, and in a few days after taken by the privateer Alexander of Salem. When near the port of Salem she was retaken by the Shannon & Tenedas frigate and ordered for Halifax, where she was about entering when she was again taken by the Y. Teazer and is at last safely moored in an American port.

The privateer Grand Turk of Salem, of 16 guns, arrived at

Portland 17th May, from a cruise. On the coast of Brazils, early in April, fell in with 2 large letter of marque ships, which she captured after a severe engagement of about 2 hours and a half. The same day captured another large ship ; they are all ordered to ———.

432. Schooner———, captured by the grand Turk privateer.

433, 434. The British packet brig Ann has arrived at Portland, captured by the privateer Yorktown of N. York ; recaptured by La Houge, 74, and again captured by the Young Teazer. And a british schooner with a cargo of fish and oil, prize to the Y. Teazer.

435, 436. Arrived at Wiscasset, privateer Thomas, Capt. Shaw, from a cruise of 1 week, with the British ship Dromo, from Liverpool for Halifax, with a cargo invoiced at *Seventy thousand pounds sterling*, and also at Boothbay a brig, cargo about 4,000 Pounds sterling. The Capt. says the above prizes are worth upwards of Six Hundred Thousand dollars.

437, 438, 439, 440. From Lloyd's List, London, April 9th, 1813. The Elizabeth Ball of Dartmouth was burnt about the middle of last month, off the Burlings by the Globe privateer of Baltimore. She has also taken an english ship from Rio Janeiro for Lisbon, laden with rice and cotton and destroyed her. A brig from Waterford bound to Newfoundland has arrived at Portsmouth, N. H., prize to the Gov. Plumer, also a brig burnt by the same privateer.

441. Arrived at New Bedford british brig Harriot,* from Buenos Ayres with a Cargo of hides, tallow, &c., prize to the privateer Brig Anaconda, Capt. Shaler of New York.

442. The privateer Anaconda captured the 17th of April, brig Packet-Express, of 12 guns, 38 men, from Rio Janeiro for London ; took from her about 6,000 Dollars in specie and gave her up to the prisoners.

443, 444, 445, 446. Arrived at Savannah, British schooner Pearl, from Curracoa for St. Croix, with corn-meal, peas, &c., captured the 11th inst., off Porto Rico, by the privateer Liberty of Baltimore, which had also taken 3 sloops, one a privateer, and gave them up to the prisoners, two being of small value and having no room for the prisoners of the third.

*Mary.

"MEMORIAL FROM THE RHODE ISLAND REGIMENT OF DRAFTED MILITIA, WAR OF 1812."

Above is the title of a pamphlet of eight octavo pages. In this memorial are set forth the claims (under an Act of Congress) of the R. I. Regiment for compensation for services rendered from August 10, 1812, to April 10, 1814.

These claims, after being duly set forth, were endorsed by the General Assembly of the State at its January Session, 1854, as follows : —

STATE OF RHODE-ISLAND AND PROVIDENCE PLANTATIONS,

In General Assembly, January Session, A. D. 1854.

Resolutions in relation to the Drafted Regiment of the War of 1812.

Resolved, That the Quota of this State called out upon the requisition of the President of the United States, under the Act of April 10th, 1812, is justly entitled to pay and allowances during the period for which it was embodied, it being from about the 10th of August, 1812, to the 10th of April, 1814, a period of about twenty months.

Resolved, That the Senators and Representatives of this State in Congress, be requested to urge on Congress the justice of making provision for the pay and allowances of the individuals composing said quota ; and that they endeavor to procure the enactment of a law, which shall place the individuals composing said quota, on the same footing in respect to pay, bounties, &c. as other State troops detached under the requisition of the President, during said war.

Resolved, That the Secretary of State is authorized to transmit these Resolutions to each of our Senators and Representatives in Congress.

A true copy—Attest,

A. POTTER, *Secretary of State.*

The memorial is signed thus : —

JOHN S. EDDY, Lieut. Colonel.
ALLEN BROWN, Quarter-Master.
BARZILLAI CRANSTON,
CALEB ARNOLD,
GEORGE LARNED,
CALEB MOSHER,
DUTY GREENE,
GEORGE READ,
DANIEL RANDALL,
JEREMIAH MUNROE,
JOSEPH DORR, and others.

In the library is another pamphlet of thirty-two pages, containing an address of thirty-four members of Congress, in 1812, to their constituents. Among the signers of this address are the names of the two representatives of this State — Richard Jackson, Jr., and Elisha R. Potter, and from Massachusetts is the name of Josiah Quincy, whose manly career caused his name to be inscribed on the roll of illustrious American citizens.

While the war of 1812 was popular neither in Rhode Island nor in other parts of New England, authentic records in this library show that this State contributed its full quota of force, on sea and land, to bring that war to a speedy conclusion. Among our manuscripts that show the part taken by Rhode Island in that war is the diary or note-book of Dr. Usher Parsons, begun September 7th, 1813, while he was serving as surgeon on board Commodore Perry's flagship, and continued while he was serving in the same position on board the Java and other U. S. frigates, till 1818. Here are also to be found references to, or rather accounts of, privateers and corsairs that sailed forth from Narragansett Bay to prey upon British commerce, far and near. The wide-spread havoc made on British vessels by these privateers, during the war, is well shown by the foregoing record of Deacon Snow.

Much light may be gained in regard to how this war was regarded in New England, by reading Theodore Dwight's "History of the Hartford Convention," found on the shelves of this library. Out of twenty-six delegates in that convention, Rhode Island had four ; viz., Daniel Lyman, Samuel Ward, Edward Manton, and Benjamin Hazard. Mr. Dwight was the secretary of that convention and his testimony published nineteen years later, in regard to its objects, merits special consideration.—[EDITOR.]

RHODE ISLAND ARTISTS.

Gilbert Stuart, while traveling in England, was asked by some of his stage-coach companions, where he was born. The artist, who was fond of mystifying inquisitive folks, answered promptly, in Narragansett, six miles from Pottowoome, ten miles from Poppasquash, and four miles from Conanicut Island. The bewildered Englishman desired to know, in what part of the East Indies that was.

In these days, especially since Blenheim House and the Marble Palace at Newport have joined hands, the average Britisher is better posted about the geography of Little Rhody.

Rhode Island has been the stamping ground for many artists of note, but the birthplace of few. Stuart and Malbone are the most celebrated of those who can claim their nativity here. Stuart was born at Narragansett in 1756 ; Malbone, at Newport in 1777. These two names alone will, perhaps, justify us in claiming that our State has raised more genius for the fine arts to the acre than any other State in the Union.

www.ingramcontent.com/pod-product-compliance
Lightning Source LLC
Chambersburg PA
CBHW021440090426
42739CB00009B/1575